CONTENTS

MOUNTAINS AND FIRE

VOLCANOES ARE TERRIFYING YET MAGNIFICENT. THE POPULAR IMAGE OF A VOLCANO IS OF A TOWERING MOUNTAIN POURING OUT MOLTEN ROCK AND SCALDING GASES. MANY VOLCANOES ARE LIKE THIS, BUT OTHERS ARE QUITE DIFFERENT.

ERUPTING VOLCANOES

Far below the surface of Earth is a layer of hot, sticky, semi-molten rock called **lava**. This rock rises to the surface and is forced out of volcanoes. It may be hurled into the sky, or ooze more gently down the sides of a mountain, setting fire to anything in its path.

21st Century Science

VOLCANOES

By Anne Rooney

ALIS

Publisher: Melissa Fairley
Editor: Miranda Smith
Designer: Emma Randall
Production Controller: Ed Green
Production Manager: Suzy Kelly

ISBN-13: 978-1-84898-103-4 pbk

Printed in China
9 8 7 6 5 4 3 2 1

Picture credits (t=top; b=bottom; c=centre; OFC= outside front cover; OBC=outside back cover)
Claus Ableiter/Wikimedia Commons (GNU 1.2): 20–21b. Bjorn Backe; Papilio/Corbis: 56–57t.
Jeremy Bishop/Science Photo Library: 35tl, 36–37. Jonathan Blair/Corbis: 16–17t. Wesley
Bocxe/Science Photo Library: 49. Corbis Photodisc: 1bl, 3D, 28l, 29r, 30l, 31r, 32l, 32r, 34l, 35r. F.
Dobran, A. Neri, M. Todesco/Science photo Library: 6-7t. Bernhard Edmaier/Science Photo Library:
59t. Mairo Fermariello/Science Photo Library: 12–13b. Arnold Fisher/Science Photo Library:
10–11. Geoeye/Science Photo Library: 34. J. D. Griggs/USGS/HVO: 40. David A. Hardy/Science
Photo Library: 14t, 27t (all). Gary Hincks/Science Photo Library: 12t, 14–15b, 17b, 28t. Istock: 1tc,
3B, 10l, 11r, 12l, 13r, 14l 15r, 16l, 17r, 18–19 all, 26, 27r, 30t, 38–39b, 46–47, 47b, 54c, 55l.
Krafft/Hoa-Qui/Science Photo Library: 58t. NASA: 1t. NASA/Carnegie Mellon University/Science
Photo Library: 29b. NASA/Science Photo Library: 51t. Courtesy of Prof. Setsuya Nakada,
University of Tokyo: 37t. New Zealand GeoNet project: 42–43. Marie-Lan Nguyen/Wikimedia
Commons: 24c. Nicholas (Nichalp)/Wikimedia Commons (cc-by-sa-2.5): 23tl. OAR/National
Undersea Research Program (NURP)/NOAA: 45t. Stephen & Donna O'Meara/Science Photo
Library: 43b. D. W. Peterson/USGS/HVO: 41b. PhotoDisc: 60. Mike Poland/Cascades Volcano
Observatory/USGS: 50l, 51. Roger Ressmeyer/Corbis: 38–39t. Alexis Rosenfeld/Science Photo
Library: 44t. Dave Sherrod/Cascades Volcano Observatory/USGS: 53b. Shutterstock: OFC, 1tl, 1tr,
1bc, 1br, 2l, 3A, 3C, 3E–G, 4–5 all, 6l, 6, 7r, 7r (background), 8–9 all, 11r (background), 17r
(background), 20l, 21r, 22 all, 22r, 24l, 24–25t, 25r (background), 31r (background), 33r
(background), 35r (background), 38l, 38r, 40l, 41r, 41r (background), 42l, 43r, 43r (background), 44l,
44r, 46l, 47r, 47r (background), 48l, 49r, 52l, 53r, 54l, 55r, 55r (background), 56l, 56–57b, 57r, 57r
(background), 58l, 59r, 59r (background), 60l, 61r, 62l, 63r, 64l, OBC all. George Steinmetz/
Corbis: 52–53. Time & Life Pictures/Getty Images: 32–33. US Geological Survey/ Science Photo
Library: 31t. Visuals Unlimited/Corbis: 20t. Howell Williams/NOAA: 33t.

The author has asserted her right to be identified as the author of this book in accordance with the
Copyright, Design and Patents Act, 1988.
The author and publisher would like to thank the following people for their help with describing their
work: Professor Chuck deMets, University of Wisconsin at Madison; Dr John Smellie, British Antarctic
Survey/University of Cambridge; Dr Andrew Jephcoat, University of Oxford; Dr Mark Sephton, Imperial
College, London; Dr Christina Heliker, Hawaiian Volcano Observatory; Dr Clive Oppenheimer, University
of Cambridge; Professor Robin Spence, University of Cambridge.

NOTE TO READERS
The website addresses are correct at the time of publishing. However, due to the ever-changing nature of
the internet, websites and content may change. Some websites can contain links that are unsuitable for
children. The publisher is not responsible for changes in content or website addresses. We advise that
internet searches should be supervised by an adult.

Some volcanoes explode into life only once in hundreds or thousands of years. Others produce smaller **eruptions** every few years, or even days. Stromboli, on an island off the coast of Sicily, puts on a display every few minutes. Violent eruptions can cause immense damage and kill thousands of people.

VOLCANOLOGY

Scientists who study volcanoes – volcanologists – brave dangerous conditions to find out why and how eruptions happen in order to help save people from their terrible effects. The event that triggered modern volcanology was the violent eruption of Krakatau in Indonesia in 1883. This gave volcanologists the first opportunity to study the stages of a major eruption and then track its aftermath and the volcano's regrowth over more than 100 years.

Erupting volcanoes are among the most spectacular – and dangerous – natural features of our planet.

A CAREER IN SCIENCE

French volcanologists Katia and Maurice Krafft worked together filming and photographing erupting volcanoes for more than 20 years. They both became interested in volcanoes as children.

A DAY IN THE LIFE OF...

Shortly after they met at Strasbourg University, the couple filmed the eruption of Stromboli, discovering that people were interested in their live coverage. The Kraffts travelled the world, visiting some of the most dangerous and exciting volcanoes and recording more than 140 eruptions – more than anyone else has done. They would often get within metres of lava flows in order to film. Their photographs remain an invaluable scientific record of such events. The Kraffts also helped to save many lives by persuading people to evacuate areas immediately threatened by eruptions. Sadly, they were both killed when a pyroclastic flow changed course while they were filming an eruption of Mount Unzen in Japan in 1991.

THE SCIENTISTS SAY...

"We would like to make it so [volcanoes] kill less people, or no people at all. And we found that by filming volcanoes very carefully and showing the risks and hazards of eruptions, this can be very useful to save lives."

CATASTROPHIC EVENTS

Volcanoes have caused catastrophes for life on Earth throughout history. Even today, despite careful monitoring of volcanoes that are known to be dangerous, disasters still happen. Some eruptions catch people unprepared, with devastating results. However, even when eruptions can be predicted, they cannot be prevented.

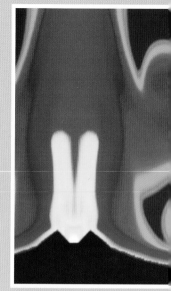

AFTER AN ERUPTION

The most spectacular effects of an eruption are the rivers or fountains of scalding molten rock – lava – that may pour from the volcano. Although it is dramatic and terrifying, lava is one of the least dangerous products of an eruption. Most lava flows quite slowly, and people can often run or even walk fast enough to keep ahead of it. Fumes, choking ash and fiery winds are much more deadly. During an eruption, tiny fragments of lava

Rising above the ruins of Pompeii, Mount Vesuvius stands as a clear reminder of the devastation that eruptions can cause.

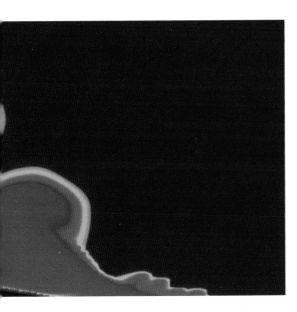

This computer simulation shows the eruption of Vesuvius in 79 CE, with the particles thrown up reaching a distance of 7km in only five minutes.

explode into clouds of volcanic ash so thick that they can block out the Sun. If ash mixes with rain, it can cause lethal floods of mud that set like concrete.

A COCKTAIL OF GASES

Worst still, volcanoes belch out fumes – gases that can be very poisonous to people, animals and plants. Sometimes a scorching wind roars out of a volcano and across the land at more than 100 km/h, roasting everything in its path. Occasionally huge chunks of solid rock are hurled from a mountainside, literally blowing it apart.

INVESTIGATING THE EVIDENCE: POMPEII 79 CE

The investigation: The town of Pompeii was destroyed by an eruption of Vesuvius in 79 CE. It was accidentally uncovered in 1689. Archaeologists have been exploring it since 1748.

The scientists: The first archaeologists were interested only in retrieving objects for collectors. Modern teams look for evidence of the Pompeiian way of life as well as details of the eruption itself. The Archaeological Superintendent of Pompeii oversees all research.

Collecting the evidence: Careful excavation of layers of ash and **pumice** has uncovered the remains of the town and its occupants, and the scientists have worked out what happened. An account written by the Roman Pliny the Younger provides invaluable evidence of the course of the disaster as well.

The conclusion: From the pattern of collapsed buildings and the state and position of the victims' bodies, it is clear that Pompeii was first hit by a rain of ash and small stones that caused buildings to collapse, and then by a searing hot wind that destroyed the town's remains and instantly killed anyone it touched.

CHAPTER ONE

A PLANET FORGED IN FIRE

VOLCANIC ERUPTIONS HAVE SHAPED OUR PLANET FOR BILLIONS OF YEARS, LONG BEFORE THERE WERE PEOPLE AROUND TO WITNESS AND RECORD THEM. THESE ERUPTIONS HELPED TO SCULPT EARTH, BRINGING GASES TO THE SURFACE AS HEAVIER MATERIALS SANK DEEPER INTO THE GROUND.

The volcano on the island of Stromboli rises 2,000m above the sea floor and has been almost continuously erupting for at least the last 2,000 years.

FORMATION OF EARTH

Earth is around 4.5 billion years old. For its first 500 million years, the young planet was scalding hot, with a surface of semi-liquid molten rock. Slowly, the heaviest materials sank towards the centre, eventually creating a core of metal. Lighter materials rose to the surface, bursting out in massive eruptions of bubbly liquid rock mixed with gases.

INSIDE EARTH

Now, after four billion years of seething activity, the planet is fairly stable and has settled into several layers. At the very centre lies an **inner core** of superheated metal as hot as the surface of the Sun, at around 6,000°C. Around this, the **outer core** is a layer of molten liquid metal that creates Earth's magnetic field. The next layer is a thick, dense blanket of semi-liquid molten rock called the **mantle**. The mantle is hot and runny deep down, but thicker and cooler near the surface. At 800–1,000°C, even the upper mantle is still very hot. The outermost layer of Earth, the **crust**, is much thinner and holds all of the planet's land and oceans. It is the only part of Earth that we know very much about. Even our most sophisticated digging and drilling equipment is not able to get below the top few kilometres of crust and into the mantle, which in most places begins 50–80km beneath the surface.

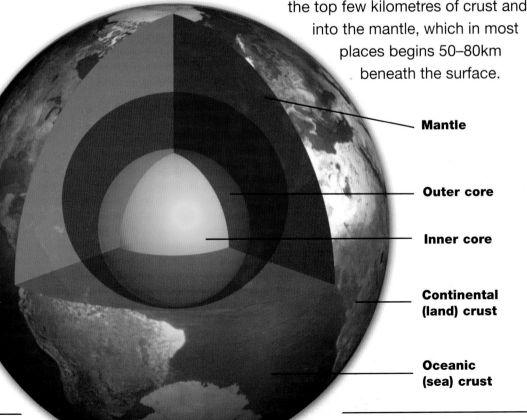

Mantle

Outer core

Inner core

Continental (land) crust

Oceanic (sea) crust

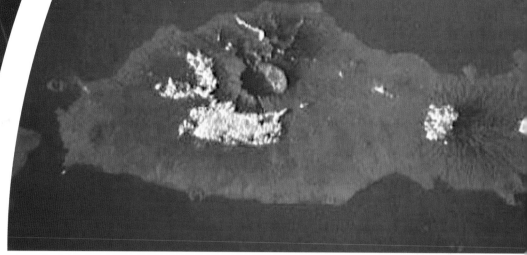

When Tambora erupted on the island of Sumbawa, Indonesia, in 1815, millions of tonnes of debris were blown around the Earth, lowering global temperatures. Snow fell in New England in June.

LAND AND AIR

Billions of years ago, volcanic activity forced huge amounts of gases trapped deep inside Earth to the surface. A toxic mix, including **ammonia**, nitrogen, carbon dioxide and **methane**, belched out of volcanoes, and Earth's **atmosphere** developed slowly. Plants and algae released more oxygen by breaking down carbon dioxide, making the air breathable for animal life. Long ago it probably brought enough water to the surface to sustain life and form the oceans. Today, lava from volcanic eruptions still contains around four per cent water. More than 1,500 volcanoes are known to have erupted in the past 10,000 years, some of them many times. There may be more that we do not know about. New volcanoes are emerging, too.

THROUGH TIME

Massive eruptions are rare in the relatively brief period of human history, and we now refer to especially large examples as super volcanoes. The last known super volcano to erupt was Toba in Indonesia, an event that took place around 73,000 years ago. It produced about a billion tonnes of debris and released about 3,000 times as much energy as the 1980 eruption of Mount Saint Helens in Washington, USA. Toba erupts at intervals of 300,000–400,000 years.

The largest eruption in recent times – and the largest in recorded history – was that of the Indonesian volcano Tambora. In 1815, it destroyed its island, blasting it apart with the force of three million atom bombs of the type dropped on Hiroshima, Japan in 1945, during World War II. The eruption resulted in the deaths of more than 90,000 people and affected the climate around the world for several years.

Natural diamonds are formed at great pressure and high temperatures deep inside the Earth's mantle.

INVESTIGATING THE EVIDENCE: INSIDE PLANET EARTH

The investigation: Scientists attempt to mimic and investigate conditions deep inside Earth and then estimate the temperature at the core and mantle.

The scientists: A team working with Dr Andrew P Jephcoat of the Department of Earth Sciences at Oxford University, UK.

Collecting the evidence: The scientists use a diamond anvil to squeeze tiny mineral samples at pressures similar to those at the centre of Earth. The anvil consists of two perfectly flat diamonds, pushed together with great force, holding a sample between them. Because diamonds are transparent, a laser can shine through them to heat the sample. By directing powerful X-rays at the mineral sample, the team reveals the arrangement of **atoms** inside it. In this way, they see how the atomic structures of minerals change under pressures as extreme as those at the centre of Earth.

The conclusion: The centre of Earth is hotter than was previously thought. The temperature of the inner core is up to 6,800°C, the outer core 5,300–5,800°C and the base of the mantle 4,300–4,800°C.

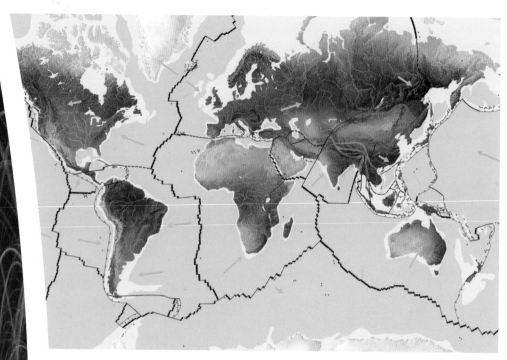

The boundaries between the Earth's tectonic plates are the sites of most of the world's volcanoes (red dots). The pink arrows show the direction of the movement of the plates.

PLATE TECTONICS

The top layer of Earth – the crust and the uppermost part of the mantle – is divided into chunks called **tectonic plates**. There are twelve large plates and several smaller ones. They float on the thick semi-molten rock of the mantle, forming a very thin solid surface.

MOVING LAND

The molten rock of the mantle seethes and circulates as hot rock rises towards the surface, cools and sinks again. The tectonic plates are carried on top, creeping slowly and making the continents move. This is called continental drift. At their boundaries, the plates push, pull or grind against each other, and volcanoes and earthquakes occur. There are three types of boundary:

Computers at volcano observatories are used to monitor volcanic activity.

- Divergent, or constructive, boundaries, where plates move in opposite directions, opening gaps in the crust.

- Convergent, or destructive, boundaries, where plates crash into each other. On land, the two plates may force rock upwards, forming huge mountain ranges. Where land and ocean meet, the heavier plate carrying the sea sinks down beneath the edge of the lighter plate carrying the land.

- Transform, or conservative, boundaries occur where plates grind against each other. As the plates get stuck, tension builds up and is released when the plates judder into movement again. **Earthquakes** may occur here.

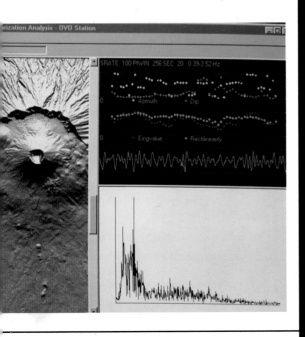

A CAREER IN SCIENCE

Professor Adam M Dziewonski is a **seismologist**. He trained in Poland as a geophysicist and is now a professor at the Department of Earth and Planetary Sciences at Harvard University in Massachusetts, USA.

A DAY IN THE LIFE OF ...

Seismologists measure and work with recordings of **seismic waves**. Seismic waves travel through the Earth, some passing over the surface and others penetrating to the core. They travel at different speeds through rock of different types and temperatures, so the inside of Earth can be mapped from a large collection of seismic data. In 1971, Professor Dziewonski proved that the inner core of Earth is solid. More recently, he has established the field of seismic **tomography**, a science that uses information calculated from seismic data to create images of the internal structure of the planet. Professor Dziewonski has also used seismic tomography to investigate the movement of tectonic plates.

THE SCIENTIST SAYS ...

"[The centre of Earth's core] may be the oldest fossil left from the formation of Earth. Its origin remains unknown, but its presence could change our basic ideas about the origin and history of the planet."

Oceanic trench

In a subduction zone, one tectonic plate slides under another. This creates an oceanic trench.

NEW LAND FOR OLD

The rock that forms the continents is very old, but the ocean floor is constantly renewed, with **magma** seeping up from the mantle at cracks located at divergent **faults**. These cracks, or **rift zones**, run down the middle of the Atlantic Ocean, through the Indian Ocean and along the eastern Pacific Ocean. The magma hardens, and as it piles up, builds great mountain ridges, taller than any found on land. The whole ocean floor edges towards the land masses. As new rock emerges in the oceans, old ocean floor meets the coast. At the border of land and sea, the heavier crust that makes up the ocean plates is forced down beneath the lighter land plates.

SUBDUCTION ZONES

The pull of old ocean floor under the land near coastlines is called subduction, and the areas where it occurs are called **subduction zones**. The old rock is pulled deep underground, where it melts. Some of the lightest rock is fed back up through volcanoes. Most land-based volcanoes are found at subduction zones, many in the countries circling the Pacific Ocean. A vast circle of volcanoes, called the Ring of Fire, runs all around the Pacific.

There are 452 volcanoes (red triangles) in the Ring of Fire that runs around the boundaries of the large Pacific tectonic plate.

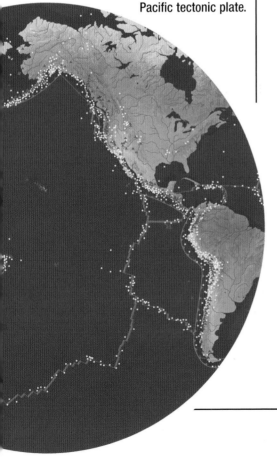

A CAREER IN SCIENCE

Chuck DeMets is a geophysicist; he studies Earth's structure, looking at the rock of the crust to investigate how tectonic plates move and geological features form. He is a professor at the University of Wisconsin–Madison, USA.

A DAY IN THE LIFE OF …

Professor DeMets uses a satellite-navigation system called **GPS** (Global Positioning System) to track ground movements around active faults and then produces 3-D computer models to show the movement of the tectonic plates. He aims to discover how Earth's crust deforms over periods from days to millions of years, and so understand the earthquake cycle. A typical field day is 15–18 hours spent preparing equipment and making measurements, usually at remote sites, as part of investigations that take any time from a few months to several years to complete. In January 2003, his team were caught in a large earthquake in Mexico. They spent two weeks taking measurements in the area to see how Earth's crust had deformed during the earthquake.

THE SCIENTIST SAYS …

"Scientific research is the most challenging and exciting job that I can imagine. We teach, travel to exotic places, discover new knowledge and hopefully leave Earth a better place than it was."

The Pearl and Hermes reef, Hawaii, is an atoll – an island that has moved away from a volcanic hot spot and is worn away by the sea.

HOT-SPOT VOLCANOES

Most volcanoes occur at plate boundaries, but a few seem to come from nowhere, appearing in the middle of tectonic plates. A line of volcanoes in the middle of a plate shows volcanic activity has happened in the same area for millions of years. These areas are called **hot spots.** The most famous chain of hot-spot volcanoes is the Hawaiian Islands. The Big Island, Hawaii, is just the last in a chain of islands that have formed over millions of years; the oldest island has already eroded and fallen beneath the waves. The plates move slowly, but the hot spot stays in the same place, and new volcanoes form as a new area of crust moves over the hot spot. Every part of Earth's surface will find itself over a volcanic hot spot around once every 500–800 million years.

GHOST VOLCANOES

When a plate moves so a volcano is no longer fed by the hot spot, the volcano **erodes**. The older Hawaiian Islands have become **atolls**. These islands are no longer volcanic but are the remnants of dead volcanoes.

▶▶ http://www.eoearth.org/article/Atoll

INVESTIGATING THE EVIDENCE: SEISMOLOGY AT A HOT SPOT

The investigation: The Hawaiian Volcano Observatory constantly monitors volcanic activity on the Hawaiian Islands. As well as being an important research centre, Hawaii attracts people who want to learn about, and witness, volcanic activity.

The scientists: A team of seismologists, geologists and other scientists working under the direction of Dr Jim Kauahikaua.

Collecting the evidence: The scientists use a network of 51 **seismometers**, most of them around the Kilauea volcano. They record around 10,000 minor earthquakes produced by volcanic activity each year. Other equipment measures changes in gravity, movement of the ground and changes in sea level. Scientists record lava and gases coming from the volcano using time-lapse photography, map new lava flows by observing them from the ground and air, analyze lava samples and monitor temperature.

The conclusion: The work reveals how magma accumulates and emerges at the Hawaiian hot spot, giving detailed records and maps of activity above and below ground.

Big Island formed when a jet of magma rose up from deep in the mantle and punched a hole in the crust.

Big Island

Earth's crust

Magma rising

CHAPTER TWO

VOLCANOES FROM THE PAST

EARTH'S LANDSCAPE PROVIDES THE BEST RECORD OF THE VOLCANIC ACTIVITY OF THE PAST. ITS DIPS AND CRACKS, TOWERING MOUNTAINS AND ROCKY COLUMNS, LAYERS OF ROCK AND BURIED FOSSILS ALL CONTAIN CLUES. VOLCANOLOGISTS AND GEOLOGISTS READ THESE – AND HUMAN ACCOUNTS THAT TELL OF MORE RECENT ERUPTIONS – TO PIECE TOGETHER THE VOLCANIC HISTORY OF EARTH.

VOLCANOES ALL AROUND

There are many areas of Earth that we no longer think of as volcanic but that are places where the landscape has been shaped by volcanoes in the distant past. Mountains, **plateaux** and towering columns of rock reveal activity in volcanoes millions of years ago.

Shiprock, in New Mexico, USA, is the eroded remains of the neck of a volcano.

The dramatic colours of the water and rock of volcanic lakes are created by bacteria. This is the Grand Prismatic Pool in Yellowstone National Park – the largest hot spring in the USA.

RIVERS OF LAVA

It might seem surprising, but a large, flat expanse of land can be the remains of a major volcanic eruption. A massive outpouring of lava that floods over the countryside, filling valleys, solidifies over millions of years into a smooth river of rock. Some of these lava rivers are vast, forming dramatic landscape features such as the Columbia River Plateau in the USA. There, between 14 and 16 million years ago, lava flooded from cracks in the ground, hardening into a layer up to 1.6km thick.

VOLCANIC SKELETONS

Often, all that remains of an old volcano is its skeleton, which is the solidified magma inside it. It stands in a column, with veins or dykes stretching outwards long after the rock of the volcano itself is worn away. The body of a volcano is formed from layers of volcanic ash compressed to make a rock called tuff. It is easily eroded and carved into shapes by wind, rain and rivers. As it erodes, it leaves behind dykes and columns of cooled magma.

CRATERS AND LAKES

Sometimes, a vast eruption blows apart a volcano or leaves a huge **crater** at the top. The space left may fill with water, forming a lake. Many crater lakes contain a poisonous mix of dissolved minerals and chemicals from the rock itself and from gases leaking from the volcano.

These strata in a sea cliff is at Oamaru, New Zealand, and shows clear layers of soft, dark grey volcanic ash. An undersea volcano erupted there 34–40 million years ago.

BURIED EVIDENCE

Past eruptions have left plenty of evidence behind. Massive volumes of lava, ash, stone and gas are hurled into the air during an eruption. They fall to Earth, and their evidence is captured for millions of years.

LAYERS OF ROCK

Many volcanoes erupt again and again, and the land around them is built up from layers of compressed ash, ejected stones and **sediment** that are laid down between eruptions. The land near volcanoes is very fertile, so plants easily grow there. As the plants die and decay, they become part of the soil. This soil eventually forms a layer of **sedimentary rock** that is distinct from the layers of ash and stone ejected from the volcano during its eruptions.

THE FOSSIL RECORD

Violent eruptions can kill all the plant and animal life in an area. Some life forms may be buried instantly under ash or stone, or under a flood of mud, and become fossilized. If the environment changes radically, different types of animals and plants may colonize the area following an eruption. The fossil record preserves these changes, and by using techniques such as **carbon dating** to discover the age of different fossils, scientists can work out what happened and when.

Although the bodies of people buried under the ash in Pompeii were not preserved, the spaces left in the hardened ash have retained their shapes. Archaeologists can produce casts of the bodies by pouring plaster or resin into the cavities.

A CAREER IN SCIENCE
Dr Gregory A Zielinski is a professor in the Department of Geosciences at the University of Massachusetts, in the USA. He examines ice-core samples in order to reveal their climatic effects.

A DAY IN THE LIFE OF ...

Ice cores are tubes of ice drilled from the permanent ice sheets of Greenland and Antarctica. As snow falls, it compacts, becoming part of the ice sheets, and trapping bubbles of air and tiny particles that were carried in the upper atmosphere. Professor Zielinksi and his team date more recent layers of ice cores by counting them like tree rings. For older layers, they look at oxygen **isotopes** in the ice and compare them with samples from known dates. They can date layers accurately up to 10,000 years ago. 'Spikes' of acidic **aerosols** and ash are evidence of eruptions. One investigation revealed a massive eruption around 73,000 years ago on the Indonesian island of Toba. It could have caused an intense volcanic winter for seven years and may have cooled Earth for 1,000 years.

THE SCIENTIST SAYS ...

"When you can look at something from different angles and see the same major result, you know you have found ... a major force on [the] Earth's climate system."

Some scientists believe that dinosaurs were wiped out by the after-effects of a massive volcanic eruption 65 million years ago.

THE END OF THEIR WORLD

Around 250 million years ago, a cataclysmic event wiped out most of the plant and animal life on land – and perhaps as much as 90 per cent of life in the sea – in a mass extinction. There have been four other mass extinctions on Earth in the past 500 million years, including the one that happened 65 million years ago, which wiped out the dinosaurs.

WORLD-SHATTERING ERUPTIONS

Volcanic eruptions often throw up enormous clouds of ash and dust that circle the globe. Sometimes, the dust is so thick that it affects the climate for many years. Larger volcanic eruptions could have the same effect – magnified many times.

Some scientists think massive eruptions may have poured lava over huge swathes of land that is now in Siberia, Russia. Around 250 million years ago, this could have caused climate and atmospheric changes severe enough to wipe out most of the life on Earth. The atmosphere

The Deccan Traps in India are step-like rock formations possibly caused by a massive eruption.

would have filled with hundreds of cubic kilometres of volcanic ash and a mist of sulphuric acid produced by sulphurous gases dissolved in water. Together, these would have blotted out light from the Sun and made the temperature plummet.

DID VOLCANOES KILL THE DINOSAURS?

Many scientists believe the effects of a meteorite hitting Earth caused the death of the dinosaurs. But some point to the huge lava fields of the Deccan Traps in India as evidence of a massive volcanic eruption that could have been responsible.

A CAREER IN SCIENCE

Dr Mark Sephton is an earth scientist at Imperial College, London, UK. He trained in geology and petroleum geochemistry.

A DAY IN THE LIFE OF …

Dr Sephton collects samples of rock and soil and analyzes them. He traces chemicals from plants and animals, using these 'molecular fossils' to find out what life was like. A huge volcanic event in Siberia, Russia, caused the climate change responsible for the mass extinction at the close of the Permian period 250 million years ago. Dr Sephton has found the remains of molecules from plants in rock laid down on the ocean floor. Traces of chemicals show that the plants were killed by acid rain and swept into the sea. Without plants to eat, land animals starved soon after. The soil had no roots to hold it in place, so it was washed into the sea, blocking out light and killing marine life.

THE SCIENTIST SAYS …

"Volcanic eruptions are not events exclusive to the geological past…. Identifying the nature of the end-Permian crisis may help us to understand what is in store for us … and better prepare how we might respond."

VOLCANOES AND PEOPLE

Volcanoes have terrified and fascinated people throughout history. Earlier societies struggled to use religion, superstition and primitive science to explain how the Earth could become so destructive.

EARLY IDEAS

Ancient Greece and Rome were both located near several volcanoes, which had an enormous impact on these civilizations. The earliest written theories to explain volcanoes were suggested by the Greek writer Thales of Miletus more than 2,500 years ago. The ancient Greeks believed that winds inside the planet fanned fires that burned sulphur. Later European thinkers shared these ideas, with only slight variations, until the 1800s.

MYTHS AND LEGENDS

In many cultures, myths and legends explain or record volcanic eruptions. In ancient Rome, people believed that if the god Vulcan – who gave his name

A bust of Vulcan, on display at the Musée du Louvre in Paris, France.

▶ ▶ http://www.mythicalrealm.com/legends/pele.html

The mythical Mount Mazama is the remains of a stratovolcano in Oregon, USA. Its collapsed caldera today holds Crater Lake.

to volcanoes – stoked his furnace too fiercely, a volcano erupted. Hawaiian myths tell of the goddess Pele causing eruptions by digging with a magic stick called Pa'oe. Her long-lasting quarrel with her sister, Namakaokahai, was said to have produced the chain of Hawaiian Islands. Sometimes, the myths, legends and art of local people provide evidence of ancient eruptions. Native Americans near Mount Mazama, in Oregon, USA, accounted for the volcano's fiery fountains by describing a war between two gods called Llao and Skell. Geological evidence has since revealed that an eruption caused the mountain to collapse 6,000 years ago.

INVESTIGATING THE EVIDENCE: DESTRUCTION OF SANTORINI

The investigation: The Greek island of Santorini, or Thera, is the horseshoe-shaped remnant of a huge volcano that erupted around 1750 BCE. It brought destruction to countries around the Mediterranean Sea, and may have been the source of the legend of the island of Atlantis. Working from ash and stone deposited by the eruption, scientists have recreated the original sequence of events.

The scientist: Professor Lionel Wilson of the Planetary Science Research Group at Lancaster University, UK, working on findings of earlier geological studies.

Collecting the evidence: Geologists have worked out the sequence of the eruption by studying the order in which ash and pumice fell on Santorini and then measuring its granule size. Professor Wilson uses mathematical formulae that he has developed to calculate exactly how tall the column of ash and gas would have been and to work out a detailed timetable for the eruption of the volcano.

The conclusion: An eruptive column of ash and lava 28–30km tall marked the first phase of the eruption, which lasted around eight hours. Then water entered the **vent** and started one or more explosions and mud flows, which lasted around 1.3 hours.

CHAPTER THREE

FROM WITHIN

VOLCANOES PROVIDE A ROUTE FOR MAGMA FROM EARTH'S MANTLE TO REACH THE SURFACE OF THE PLANET, WHETHER IN OCCASIONAL VIOLENT BURSTS OR IN A SLOW AND STEADY TRICKLE MAINTAINED OVER YEARS OR CENTURIES. THE WAY IN WHICH VOLCANOES ERUPT DETERMINES HOW THEY GROW AND WHAT THEY EVENTUALLY LOOK LIKE.

TYPES OF VOLCANO

The classic shape of a mountain with a crater at the top is not the only type of volcano. Some volcanoes do not look like mountains at all, and others are broken and irregular, battered out of shape by their own violent activity.

Volcanologists have classified volcanoes in three main groups – shield volcanoes, cinder cones and stratovolcanoes – although there are others. The volcanoes are grouped according to their shape, the materials they are made of and the way in which the volcano erupts.

Mauna Loa, Hawaii, is a shield volcano and is the largest volcano on Earth, covering an area of 75,000 cu.km!

There are three types of crater. The hornito (left) is small and narrow and formed by explosions of lava, so the lava is molten when it lands. The maars (centre) is usually up to 1km wide and is formed explosively when ground water comes into contact with magma. The cinder cone crater (right) throws lava high into the air where it solidifies before falling as ash and rock.

SHIELD VOLCANOES

Shield volcanoes, like those of the Hawaiian Islands, are vast, gently sloping domes kilometres long. These volcanoes form when lava from **fissures** in the ground oozes out over a long period. Although they do not look like mountains, the islands of Hawaii are formed of the tallest volcanoes in the world. The biggest, Mauna Loa, rises 8,700m from the ocean floor to its summit. Lava erupts gently and shield volcanoes are rarely dangerous.

CINDER CONES

A cinder cone, or scoria cone, is a classic volcano shape. Lava pours from the central vent, often blasted far into the air, where it breaks into small fragments that solidify. It falls to the ground as ash and rock, piling up into a cone shape, usually with a bowl-shaped crater at the summit. Cinder cones are usually under 1,000m tall and grow quickly over a short period of eruptions. They then die and erode slowly.

STRATOVOLCANOES

Stratovolcanoes, or composite volcanoes, are much bigger than cinder cones and form over hundreds or thousands of years. They are steep-sided and symmetrical. They have a central vent, and often additional vents and cracks that also erupt lava. Their eruptions are violent and dangerous, and sometimes vast chunks of the volcano are blown away. Enormous volumes of ash and dust sweep down the slopes. After each eruption, they regrow gradually from within.

This cutaway shows the internal structure of a stratovolcano, with magma rising up through the central conduit and out through the vent to pour down the sides of the mountain. Magma is also forced out of smaller vents and cracks in the sides of the volcano.

ANATOMY OF A VOLCANO

Although volcanoes are different shapes, they all share some basic features. They are fed magma from deep underground and bring it to the surface through one or more channels.

COLLECTING MAGMA

Every volcano is fed by a magma chamber, a pool of magma that has risen from the mantle to collect underground, far beneath the volcano. As more magma rises, the magma chamber grows, melting the rock around it and sometimes distorting the ground above. From the chamber, magma makes its way to the surface by travelling up a channel called a **conduit**. This can be 30m across and stretch many kilometres from the magma chamber. The end of the conduit is at the vent, which is the opening of the volcano at the surface.

▶▶ www.cosmeo.com/braingames/virutal_volcano/index.cfm?title=
Virtual Volcano

Magma does not only travel straight up the conduit to the central vent. Often, there are dykes that emerge in smaller vents and cracks on the sides of the mountain.

ALL QUIET

When a volcano is not erupting, the vent and conduit are usually blocked with a plug of old volcanic rock. This is magma that has hardened at the end of an eruption, or rock that has fallen back into the vent when parts of the volcano have been blasted away by an eruption.

The Dante II robot explores the crater of Mount Spurr, an active volcano in Alaska, USA, in 1994.

A CAREER IN SCIENCE

Dante II is a robotic volcanologist, created by Carnegie Mellon University in Pennsylvania, USA, and NASA to investigate live volcanoes. The robot goes into areas and environments that are too dangerous for people to explore.

A DAY IN THE LIFE OF ...

In 1994, Dante's work involved walking into the crater of the live volcano Mount Spurr in Alaska to take photographs and collect gas and rock samples. Dante was tethered to a cable and climbed down the steep crater wall, negotiating loose rock, ash and ice. Although it narrowly missed being crushed by several careening boulders, Dante reached the crater floor to send back video footage and collect samples. On the way back out, the robot slipped and tipped over. During a helicopter rescue, Dante fell again and was severely damaged, but was finally airlifted out. Dante is now retired and tours the United States as part of a robotics exhibition.

A SCIENTIST SAYS ...

"A robot can be made to withstand lots of heat, cold, smoke and other harsh conditions. One of the neatest aspects of a robot is that it can dwell and take samples for many days or even weeks and months..." – John Bares, head of the Dante II project at Carnegie Mellon University

Edinburgh Castle in Scotland sits on Castle Rock, part of the remains of an extinct volcano.

THE GROWING VOLCANO

A volcano develops as lava, ash and stones start piling up from its first eruption. Lava may ooze out and harden, or be blasted into the air and scattered, stacking into a mountain.

BETWEEN ERUPTIONS

Some volcanoes erupt almost constantly, with gentle bursts of activity every few years, months or even days. Others erupt at intervals of centuries or millennia, and some perhaps on cycles of millions of years. Usually, the volcanoes that have the most dangerous eruptions erupt least frequently, having more time to build up a large store of magma. While a volcano is capable of erupting, it is described as **live**. There may be long intervals between eruptions, when it is said to be **dormant**.

DEAD OR SLEEPING?

When a volcano is no longer able to erupt, it is described as extinct. It can be difficult to tell whether a volcano is truly extinct or whether

Part of Mount St Helens in Washington, USA, was blown away by an eruption in 1980.

it is just dormant. Very old volcanoes that have not erupted for thousands of years, and that have no trace of hot magma, are classified as extinct – but some may still surprise us.

CHANGING SHAPE

The shape of a volcano may change over time as rock is eroded by the wind, weather, water and ice. This can happen between eruptions or after the volcano is dead. Between eruptions, the mountain may also grow and change as magma wells up from beneath. Sometimes, major eruptions blow away part or even all of the mountain, or it collapses into its own emptied magma chamber.

INVESTIGATING THE EVIDENCE: WHEN WILL MOUNT TARANAKI ERUPT AGAIN?

The investigation: Mount Taranaki, on the North Island of New Zealand, is the second largest volcano in the country. There are no human records of past volcanic activity taking place there. Scientists have examined fallout from previous eruptions and this has helped them to work out how often the volcano erupts.

The scientists: Dr Shane Cronin of the Institute of Natural Resources at Massey University, New Zealand, and PhD student Michael Turner.

Collecting the evidence: The researchers drilled into the bed of a lake near the volcano to extract samples of sediment. Analyzing these, they found more than 100 layers of ash and pumice had been deposited over thousands of years. These products of earlier eruptions give a hint of what we may expect in the future.

The conclusion: Mount Taranaki has erupted at least once every 90 years for the past 9,000 years, and has a major eruption every 500 years. Its last major eruption was in 1655, and there has been no eruption for 200 years, so one is probably overdue.

A VOLCANO FROM NOWHERE

A peaceful cornfield in Mexico was the site of one of the most remarkable births of the 20th century. Parícutin, a brand-new volcano, gave volcanologists the chance to watch a volcano grow from nothing, erupt and then die in only a few years.

RISING MOUND

Dionisio and Paula Pulido were burning shrubs on their farm on 20 February 1943 when the ground in front of them began to rise up and crack, opening into a 2.5m fissure that belched fumes and smoke. In less than 24 hours, a 50m-high cinder cone had grown, erupting chunks of lava that fell as small stones. By the end of the week, the new volcano was 100m tall and raining ash onto the nearby village.

INCREASED VIGOUR

The activity of the new volcano grew more powerful, and soon it produced columns of ash and gas several kilometres tall. Pouring lava and ash falls affected nearby settlements, and the village of Parícutin itself was swamped with lava, leaving only the church towers unaffected.

The volcanic island of Surtsey is 32km from the southern coast of Iceland.

DYING DOWN

After its rapid burst of activity, Parícutin slowed down and eventually stopped erupting altogether in 1952. It grew little in its last years, leaking lava from the base of the cone instead. Its final height was 424m. It will slowly wear away as erosion takes its toll.

Local villagers watch the smoke cloud forming following the eruption of Parícutin in 1943.

INVESTIGATING THE EVIDENCE: A VOLCANIC BIRTH

The investigation: At the mid-Atlantic rift zone that stretches through Iceland, new land is created by volcanic activity. Between 1963 and 1967, the birth of a new island, Surtsey, gave volcanologists the chance to watch the process.

The scientists: Scientific groups from Iceland and around the world studied the emergence of Surtsey.

Collecting the evidence: The eruption was first noticed in November 1963. After only ten days, a new island 900 x 650m had emerged. Scientists observed and filmed the growth of the island, taking samples of gas and lava over the three and a half years of activity. Once the volcanic activity had stopped, biologists and botanists tracked the development of the island as a new habitat, observing its colonization first by mosses and lichen and then by plants, insects, birds and animals.

The conclusion: By analyzing the samples and data collected, the volcanologists built up a timetable. First, lava leaked onto the ocean floor. Then eruptions became more explosive, and large piles of volcanic rock built up. When the volcano was tall enough to prevent sea water entering the vent, the eruptions became less violent. Flows and fountains of lava glued together the loose matter, making the island secure against the sea.

DEATH AND REGROWTH

While cinder cones such as Parícutin in Mexico have a brief period of eruptive activity and then die and erode away slowly, shield volcanoes and stratovolcanoes erupt again and again over a much longer period. When they are quiet, or dormant, they provide a rich environment for living things.

REGROWTH AND REGENERATION

Volcanic ash becomes fertile soil, and lush plant growth soon attracts insects, birds and animals to a quiet volcano. Many human societies have developed near volcanoes because the fertile soil is easy to farm and produces abundant crops. It takes only a short time for an area devastated by an eruption to be recolonized by plants and wildlife.

Anak Krakatau is the youngest island in the Krakatau group. It emerged about 80 years ago, and the plant life that has floated or been blown there is only just beginning to establish itself (right).

▶ ▶ http://www.geology.sdsu.edu/how_volcanoes_work/Krakatau.html

Volcanic soil is very fertile, and easy to farm, so people like to live near volcanoes.

Sadly, a new eruption may quickly wipe out the new life establishing itself on the volcano's slopes.

A VOLCANO REFORMS

While plants and animals move in above the ground, magma collects again in the chamber beneath. There may be no outward sign of this for years or even centuries. Sometimes, the mountain begins to bulge and swell, or grows new outcrops of rock as things move underneath. A new cone may grow inside the old crater, or small **lava domes**, like miniature volcanoes, spring up on the slopes.

INVESTIGATING THE EVIDENCE: WATCHING KRAKATAU

The investigation: The Indonesian volcano Krakatau blew apart in 1883, destroying every living thing on the island. Scientists have tracked the reappearance of plants and animals there.

The scientists: Beginning in 1884, Dutch scientists began to study the re-emergence of the island's **ecosystem**. The study of plant growth is continuing today under Mark Bush, an assistant professor of zoology at Ohio State University, USA.

Collecting the evidence: From 1884 to 1930, scientists noted the arrival of every new **species** of plant and animal. Today, Bush's team has tagged many of the individual trees on the island, allowing them to trace the arrival of new specimens and record the growth and death of the trees that have already appeared.

The conclusion: So far Krakatau's rainforest has only 80 species – just 10 per cent of the variety of living things that it should have. This reveals that it takes a rainforest far longer to recover from a disaster than scientists thought previously. The information has implications for human exploitation of rainforests in other parts of the world.

CHAPTER FOUR

IT'S TIME!

VOLCANOES ARE AT THEIR MOST EXCITING – AND DEADLY – WHEN THEY ARE ERUPTING. AN ERUPTION IS AN EXHILARATING TIME FOR VOLCANOLOGISTS, AND A SIGNIFICANT ERUPTION ATTRACTS SCIENTISTS FROM AROUND THE WORLD. HOWEVER, IT CAN HAVE TERRIBLE EFFECTS FOR THE PEOPLE WHO LIVE NEAR THE VOLCANO.

GETTING READY

Though a volcano may lie dormant for many years, it eventually bursts into life again. There is often some warning before an eruption – rumbling, earthquakes or gas pouring from the crater. But not all volcanoes give such useful signs.

MAGMA BUILD-UP

The magma chamber swells as more and more magma rises into it. As the pressure intensifies, magma begins to force its way towards the surface, pouring up the conduit towards the vent, and leaking into the body of the mountain through

Gas and smoke escape from the summit craters of Mount Etna on the Italian island of Sicily. Etna's continual gentle activity produces regular small lava flows and the release of gases.

Scientists drill into the Unzen volcano in Japan to learn about the processes that lead to an eruption.

dykes. The ground may swell and become warm, and gas escapes through cracks and holes called fumaroles. Scientists watching the volcano collect gas for analysis and use laser-measurement techniques to see how the shape of the ground changes. With thermal imaging, they can study the volcano's changing temperature profile.

GRUMBLES AND RUMBLES

Rumbles and loud bangs often give warning that a volcano is getting ready to erupt. The noises are produced by pockets of gas escaping as the magma nears the surface, or by cracking rocks. If people living nearby know how to interpret the sounds, they will have time to leave the area safely before the eruption begins.

MELTING UNDER PRESSURE

As more magma rising from below presses into that which has already collected and cannot escape, the pressure within the volcano becomes immense. It starts to melt the surrounding rock of the mountain. The amount of magma increases in the magma chamber, conduit and dykes, pushing upwards towards the vent.

Dr Christina Heliker shields her face as she collects red-hot pahoehoe lava during an eruption of the Kilauea volcano in Hawaii.

FIERY CATACLYSM

When an eruption finally starts, exactly what happens depends on the type of volcano and the composition of the lava.

MAGMA AND GAS

Not all magma is the same. Some has a lot of dissolved water and is very runny; it may pour in rivers down a slope. Thicker lava with less water oozes like toothpaste from a tube and piles up near a vent or slides slowly down the slopes of a volcano. Gas stays dissolved in the magma until the pressure or temperature drops. Then it forms bubbles, and the volume of the magma increases massively, forcing it to explode from the volcano. The more gas the magma

▶ ▶ www.soest.hawaii.edu/GG/HCV/puuoo_history.html

contains, the more violently it erupts. Thick magma containing a lot of gas leads to explosive and dangerous eruptions. Thin lava full of gas produces spectacular fountains, or large curtains of fire.

This close-up of basalt rock clearly shows the bubbles that are formed by gas.

A CAREER IN SCIENCE

Dr Christina Heliker is a volcanologist who works at the Hawaiian Volcano Observatory. She first studied glaciers, but when Mount St Helens, in Washington, USA, erupted in 1980, she volunteered to help and was quickly converted to volcanology.

A DAY IN THE LIFE OF …

Dr Heliker works with two other geologists to map and monitor eruptions in Hawaii. Day by day, she builds up a detailed account of the lava flows. She works extensively on the ground at the Pu'u 'O'o vent of the Kilauea volcano. To get more data, she also uses a helicopter to fly dangerously close to the erupting fissures. Whenever she is near the volcano, she has to wear heatproof clothing and a gas mask to protect her from the fumes. As well as working in the field, Dr Heliker uses computers to analyze her findings and work out what they reveal about the volcano's activity.

THE SCIENTIST SAYS …

"Usually geologists are studying landscapes that took thousands or millions of years to form, and out here in Hawaii we can see drastic changes from day to day. So volcanoes are very powerful places to work. An active volcano almost feels like a living entity."

In this Hawaiian eruption, fountains of lava flow down the sides of the Pu'u 'O'o crater on the southeast rift zone of Kilauea.

TYPES OF ERUPTION

Some volcanoes produce violent and dangerous eruptions, while others are more gentle. Plinian eruptions, like that which destroyed the ancient Roman town of Pompeii in 79 CE, are among the most dangerous. They are highly explosive, shooting vast clouds of ash and gas many kilometres into the sky, and can continue for days. Chunks of lava solidify and fall to the ground as small stones and ash. Hawaiian eruptions do not often involve much gas. Instead the lava pours or oozes down the slopes. This type can be more gaseous and produce dramatic spurting fountains, but there are no clouds of ash and gas, and they are rarely dangerous. Strombolian eruptions are named after the volcano Stromboli off the coast of Sicily. They are not dangerous and are usually short-lived. They throw out showers or fountains of lava, but they produce little ash and lava rarely flows down the sides of the volcano. Vulcanian eruptions produce a column of gas and ash and can hurl chunks of lava into the sky. These lava 'bombs' harden into rock and can be dangerous as they crash to the ground. There is usually no lava flow.

SOLID LAVA

Tiny round stones, called lapilli, are droplets of lava that have solidified. They are full of trapped gas from the bubbles in the lava. Thicker lava that has crawled along the ground hardens more slowly. The inside of a large lava flow can stay hot for years even though the outside is cold and hard. The rock it makes is brittle, filled with pockets of air and has razor-sharp edges.

'Pele's hair' describes the volcanic glass threads formed when molten material is spun in the wind.

INVESTIGATING THE EVIDENCE: THE GEOLOGY OF ERUPTIONS ON HAWAII

The investigation: Geologists on Hawaii study the products of present and past eruptions, working out the make-up of the lava involved.

The scientists: Scientists at the Hawaiian Volcano Observatory, including Christina Heliker (see pages 38–39).

Collecting the evidence: Geologists take samples of past eruptions from the solidified lava deposits around the islands. The lava flow of current eruptions is measured using GPS (Global Positioning System) equipment, and photos and video taken from the air. By studying the minerals and chemicals present, scientists find out about the conditions inside the volcano. They use this information to identify and forecast dangers to local people.

The conclusion: The results of these studies help to reveal how Hawaiian volcanoes erupt, how magma moves up from deep underground, what causes explosive eruptions and the physical and chemical changes that take place in magma and lava.

FIRES, FLOODS AND FUMES

The products of an eruption can include a combination of liquid or sticky lava, falling rocks and small stones, clouds of ash, gas and scorching winds. An eruption can also set off other events that can be just as devastating for human communities as the eruption itself.

SCORCHING WINDS

A scalding wind of superheated gases called a **pyroclastic flow** is one of the most dangerous effects of an eruption. Pyroclastic flows travel at 100 km/h or more, with temperatures up to 1,000°C. These winds roar down a mountainside, incinerating everything. People die instantly, and trees, plants and houses are turned to carbon.

MUDSLIDES AND AVALANCHES

Many eruptions are accompanied by terrible rainstorms, and some blast through lakes and rivers. The combination of water and volcanic ash can be disastrous, as huge mudslides pour down

This lahar – a flood made up of pyroclastic material and water – is flowing down the mountainside at the Whakapapa ski resort, Mount Ruapehu, in New Zealand.

▶ ▶ http://volcanoes.usgs.gov/ash/

a mountainside and swamp towns and villages. The mud, often metres thick, sets like concrete. In snowy regions, eruptions can set off avalanches, sending massive sheets of snow sliding downhill.

ASH AND GASES

The ash from an eruption cloud can fall over a large area, choking people and animals and blocking the engines of aeroplanes and other vehicles. In some areas, an ash fall may be metres deep. Poisonous fumes can also sweep over the countryside. After the eruption of the Icelandic volcano Laki in 1783, more than 10,000 people died of starvation when poisonous gases destroyed farmland and animals.

The village of Bilbao was destroyed by an ash fall after the eruption of the Tungurahua volcano in Ecuador in 2006.

INVESTIGATING THE EVIDENCE: IN FULL FLOW

The investigation: When a lahar poured down Mount Ruapehu in New Zealand in 2006, a research team from Massey University rushed to the scene.

The scientists: Three teams of volcanologists, including 17 postgraduate students led by Dr Shane Cronin, director of the Volcanic Risk Solutions Group, and Dr Vern Manville of the Institute of Geological and Nuclear Sciences.

Collecting the evidence: Researchers moved in ahead of the lahar to plant seismometers in its path. This was the first time that seismometers had been used to reveal the internal dynamics of a flowing lahar, and they revealed invaluable information. In addition, researchers observed the flow and took samples of the water and sediment. After the lahar was over, they carried out an aerial survey using laser technology, and took 83,000 measurements. These were used to build a 3-D model of the channel created by the lahar, which was compared to the model of the area made earlier.

The conclusion: The lahar was found to travel at a top speed of 35km/h. The investigation showed that a predictive model of lahars that had been prepared beforehand was mostly accurate. Although this lahar was not triggered by volcanic activity, the information collected will help to plan for future volcanic events.

A diver records the surface temperatures at the crater of the submerged volcano Ferdinandea. Research shows that this volcano, about 30km south of the Italian island of Sicily, may erupt again soon, and that this would cause it to emerge above sea level.

ALL AT SEA

There are more volcanoes under the sea than there are on land – perhaps as many as 20,000 – and most of them have never been mapped or examined by scientists.

UNDERSEA VOLCANOES

Volcanoes form under the sea when tectonic plates move apart and are the source of the magma that becomes the rock of the new ocean floor. They are usually fissure volcanoes, like those on the Hawaiian Islands – cracks that open in the ground with lava leaking out. Lava solidifies almost immediately underwater, creating a glassy sheet rather than the lumpy or brittle lava common on and near land-based volcanoes.

VENTS AND SMOKERS

Near the rift zones under the sea, holes in the ocean floor leak gases at high temperatures. Minerals from the gases dissolve in the surrounding water, or crystallize to form towering columns that

▶▶ www.pbs.org/wgbh/nova/abyss/life/

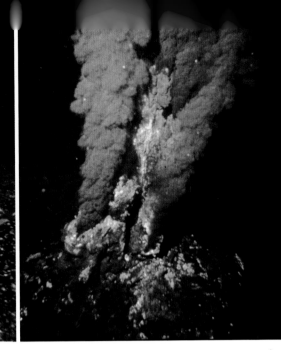

Black smokers give off volcanic gases at a mid-ocean ridge. These vents pour out sulphurous, mineral-rich fluid.

A CAREER IN SCIENCE

Dr John R Delaney is a professor of oceanography at the University of Washington, USA. He studies deep-sea vents and the unusual forms of life that inhabit them.

A DAY IN THE LIFE OF ...

Dr Delaney's fieldwork takes place in the middle of the ocean on a ship. His team uses a robotic submersible – a craft that travels down to some of the deepest parts of the ocean, with no onboard pilot. Controlled by computer from the ship, the submersible uses a chainsaw and other tools to gather samples from black smokers and vents. These sample are then analyzed and examined in a laboratory. Sea vents are one of the last unexplored habitats on Earth. Studying them could reveal vital insights into how life may have started on Earth. They show us for the first time the type of life forms that can exist without sunlight, in water that is at temperatures up to 400°C and is full of dissolved acids and minerals. They may even show us how life could exist on other planets, with conditions unlike those on Earth.

THE SCIENTIST SAYS ...

"One of my great dreams ... is that our understanding of the submarine systems here on Earth will guide us unerringly to the discovery of life elsewhere."

become funnels for the volcanic gases. These rocky towers are called black or white 'smokers', depending on their colour. They grow quickly but are fragile and break off easily. Smokers provide a habitat for many organisms and micro-organisms that are found nowhere else on Earth. Able to survive in extreme temperatures and acidic conditions, these creatures are highly specialized, with bodies that depend on using sulphur rather than oxygen. They range from tiny microbes that live inside volcanic vents to giant tube worms and glowing crabs that colonize the outside of the smokers.

TSUNAMI!

Volcanic eruptions under or near the sea can be particularly explosive in character. If cold water and hot magma meet, a violent eruption often occurs, with the sudden chilling of the magma and heating of the sea water causing a massive expansion that blows the volcano apart. These are called phreatomagmatic eruptions and can lead to devastating results.

EXPLOSIVE MIX

When an island, underwater or coastal volcano blows apart, the sea often rushes into the space left behind. This can trigger a tsunami. This is a gigantic wave that is set in motion by the displacement of a large body of water. Even if the sea water does not come into contact with the magma or lava, massive chunks of rock falling into the sea can be enough to set off a tsunami.

KILLER WAVES

Unlike ordinary waves, which move only the surface water, tsunami move a vast body of water from the surface to the ocean floor. Out at sea, a tsunami is only around 1m tall and is barely noticeable, but it travels at great speed. As it approaches land, however, the tsunami slows down and grows much taller. When it hits the coast, it sweeps inland as a flood up to 30m deep, swamping everything in its path.

A tsunamis travels at over 800km/h across the open sea. It slows as it approaches land but increases in height, resulting in a devastating impact on coastal areas.

The sea sweeps back out once the wave has passed, pulling with it everything that has been caught up by the tsunami. When Krakatau in Indonesia erupted in 1883, few people died in the eruption itself, but 36,000 people were killed by the tsunami that flooded coastal areas and islands in the Indian Ocean.

With no advance warning, a tsunami can completely destroy whole communities, leaving behind it a high death toll. About 80 per cent of all tsunamis happen in the Pacific Ocean.

INVESTIGATING THE EVIDENCE: PREDICTING TSUNAMIS

The investigation: Scientists mapping the volcanic island of La Palma in the Canary Islands, off the coast of North Africa, have discovered that an eruption could trigger a mega tsunami that would cross the Atlantic Ocean, devastating parts of Europe and the USA.

The scientists: A team under Dr Simon Day of the Benfield Hazard Research Centre at University College, London, UK, has been working with computer-modelling experts at the Swiss Federal Institute of Technology in Zurich, Switzerland.

Collecting the evidence: Dr Day has revealed that the east and west halves of the volcano are slowly separating. One day an eruption will break the island apart, throwing 500 billion tonnes of rock into the sea. Computer models show that a tsunami tens of metres tall will sweep out in circles, affecting Western Europe and crossing the Atlantic to North America and the Caribbean.

The conclusion: The tsunami will happen, but no one can tell when. Dr Day says the chances of it occurring in any particular century are one in 20. Even if there is a warning before the next eruption occurs, we are unlikely to know in advance if it will cause the island's collapse.

VOLCANOES AND CLIMATE CHANGE

Climate change is headline news, with most scientists believing that human activity is responsible for rising global temperatures. But it is not only people who can change the weather – volcanoes have an effect, too, both raising and reducing the temperature.

GETTING WARMER ...

Rising global temperatures are related to people's use of **fossil fuels** such as coal, oil and natural gas, which release carbon dioxide into the atmosphere. Volcanoes also emit carbon dioxide as well as other greenhouse gases. However, in an average year humans are responsible for 99 per cent of emissions and volcanoes for only one per cent.

... AND COOLER

Major volcanic eruptions throw huge volumes of ash and gas into the atmosphere. Ash sometimes blocks the Sun completely for days in areas close to an eruption. However, tiny suspended droplets of sulphuric acid, caused by sulphurous gases dissolving in water in the air, have a far greater effect on the weather. They reflect heat back out into space, lowering the temperature on Earth. After the eruption of the Indonesian volcano Tambora in 1815, Europe suffered a 'year without a summer' in 1816 – snow and frost struck Britain even in June, July and August. The eruption of Krakatau in Indonesia in 1883 caused temperatures to drop for several months, and when Mount Pinatubo in Chile erupted in 1991, global temperatures fell by 1°C.

The Popocatépetl volcano is the second highest peak in Mexico. When it erupted in 1994, it had been dormant for about 60 years. The column of ash and gas rises several kilometres into the sky each time it erupts.

▶▶ www.geology.sdsu.edu/how_volcanoes_work/climate_effects.html

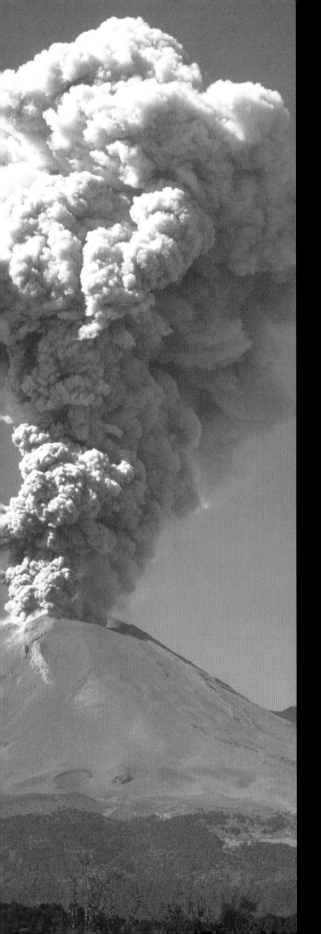

A CAREER IN SCIENCE

Dr John Smellie is a volcanologist working for the British Antarctic Survey in Antarctica and Cambridge, UK. His research looks at how volcanoes and ice sheets interact and how the record of past ice sheets can be worked out from volcanic evidence preserved in Antarctica.

A DAY IN THE LIFE OF ...

Dr Smellie studies volcanoes that erupted through ice sheets millions of years ago, and some that are still erupting today. He gathers rock and sediment samples, and recently observed an ice-covered erupting volcano from a plane. In Antarctica, his expeditions last two or three months, travelling by quad motorbike or skidoo. Back in the UK, he dates the rock samples and analyzes them to discover their geochemical composition. From this information he can reconstruct when and where ice sheets existed in the past and discover many of their most important features.

THE SCIENTIST SAYS ...

"I work in a region that very few others have seen, including places where I am certain no others have visited. That my work in the geological past can help us to understand the shape of our planet's environmental future is deeply satisfying."

CHAPTER FIVE

EYE IN THE SKY

SCIENTISTS KEEP A CAREFUL WATCH ON VOLCANOES AROUND THE WORLD, ESPECIALLY THOSE THAT ARE CLOSE TO INHABITED AREAS. SOME CITIES, SUCH AS TOKYO IN JAPAN AND NAPLES IN ITALY, LIE IN THE SHADOW OF DANGEROUS VOLCANOES AND HAVE SUFFERED THE EFFECTS OF PAST ERUPTIONS. ANY INDICATION OF A COMING ERUPTION COULD HELP TO SAVE LIVES BECAUSE PEOPLE COULD BE EVACUATED IN TIME.

SATELLITES

The work of scientists studying volcanoes has changed since the invention of planes and satellites. It is much easier to get a view of a large structure like a volcano from above. Indeed, some volcanoes were not even recognized until it became possible to see them from the air. Satellites carry cameras and imaging equipment and are used for measuring positions on Earth's surface with great precision.

of large areas of land can be easily measured using satellites and GPS technology. A GPS receiver on Earth picks up signals transmitted by the satellites and is able to work out its exact position. Volcanologists place GPS receivers on and around volcanoes. As the ground deforms and moves, the positions of the GPS receivers shift. By tracking the movement of the receivers scientists are able to map the movement of the ground.

TWISTED LAND

As magma builds up inside a volcano, the ground above often changes shape. This distortion is called **deformation**. Deformation

HOT ROCK WITHIN

Infrared imaging is used to create a map of temperature gradients within objects or landscapes. Infrared cameras installed on satellites or carried on planes can take a series of images of a volcano to show how the temperature on and under the ground changes over time. These images are used by scientists to identify hot spots where magma is collecting or rising to the surface. They can warn volcanologists of increased volcanic activity.

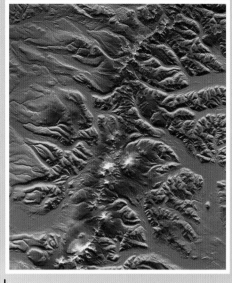

This map of the Sredinnyy Khrebet volcanoes, Russia, was made by radar equipment on the Space Shuttle *Endeavour*.

A geologist sets up a Global Positioning Station (GPS) on the east flank of Mount St Helens, Washington, USA, to measure deformation of the ground that may accompany a swarm of earthquakes.

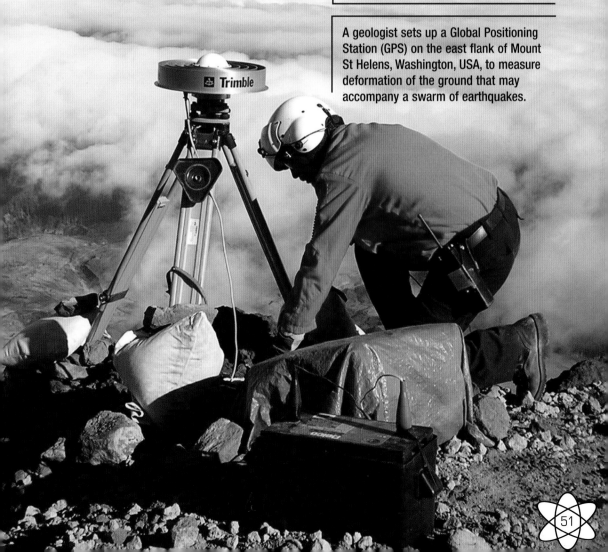

ON THE GROUND

Not all the work monitoring volcanoes can be done from a safe distance. There is still a need for volcanologists to be on the ground, dangerously close to a volcano that is about to erupt.

CLUES IN GASES

Many volcanoes leak small amounts of gas from their crater and fumaroles. An increase in the amount of gas or a change in its composition can be an early warning sign that more activity is likely. Volcanologists go onto the volcano, and into the crater while the volcano is quiet, to collect gas samples and record temperatures.

MOVING GROUND

As magma builds up, the ground shifts. Volcanoes are surveyed using laser-measuring equipment that is extremely accurate. Tiltmeters show if the ground is shifting vertically and extensometers show if it is shifting horizontally as cracks widen or shrink. Under the sea,

The summit of Mt Erebus, the most active volcano in Antarctica, is littered with volcanic bombs from eruptions.

pressure recorders reveal any change in the underwater pressure caused by the ocean floor rising or sinking as magma moves below. Movement deep underground does not always translate to movement on the surface. As more and more magma collects, it puts pressure on the rock of the volcano causing it to break, or makes cracks that are already there vibrate. This produces swarms of tiny earthquakes. Seismometers measure vibrations passing through Earth. Many are solar-powered and transmit their readings directly to computers in distant observatories.

Scientists install a new tiltmeter on Mount St Helens volcano, in Washington, USA. Tiltmeters are used to predict very small changes from the horizontal, and often monitor volcanoes.

A CAREER IN SCIENCE
Clive Oppenheimer works in volcanology and remote sensing at Cambridge University, UK.

A DAY IN THE LIFE OF ...
Dr Oppenheimer spends most of his time in Antarctica, Italy, Central America and Ethiopia, where he measures gas coming from live volcanoes. The exact mixture of different gases leaking from the magma reveals the likelihood of a volcanic eruption and what type of eruption to expect. To measure gas emissions from a distance, Dr Oppenheimer uses a computer-controlled device called a spectrometer, which is connected to a telescope so that he can see the gas clouds. A laptop processes the data, giving instant readings of the composition of the gases. He can even measure the gases being released from violent explosions, when it would be impossible to get close.

THE SCIENTIST SAYS ...
"One of the great things about volcanology is that anyone can get involved in it – volcanoes affect the environment, climate, society; tell us about the inside of the earth, other planets and moons, even the origins of life and the causes of extinctions. Mathematicians, physicists, geologists, climate experts, anthropologists, archaeologists, doctors, emergency planners – the list is endless – all get involved...."

SUPER VOLCANO

Super volcanoes erupt with terrifying force, causing local devastation and lasting effects worldwide. The last super volcano to erupt was Toba in Indonesia around 73,000 years ago. There is a super volcano lurking beneath Yellowstone National Park in the USA, which could erupt at any time in the next 50,000 years. It is carefully monitored by a team of scientists.

SECRET MOUNTAIN

Yellowstone was not recognized as a **caldera** until it was seen from the air in 1872. On the ground, it covers such a vast area that its shape is hidden. The caldera at Yellowstone is the most recent of three hot-spot volcanoes that have grown and erupted in the area in the last two billion years. On the ground, clues to its volcanic nature are hot springs, **geysers** and boiling mud pools, all fuelled by the hot magma only 6km below the surface.

A DISASTER WAITING TO HAPPEN

Eruptions in the Yellowstone area have happened at intervals of 650,000–800,000 years, and it has been 640,000 years since the last one. The volcano is unlikely to erupt in the very near future, but when it does, the thousands of cubic kilometres of magma gathered beneath the park will emerge with such force that the whole of the USA will be covered with ash and the

Bacteria that live in different temperatures colour the Grand Prismatic Spring in Yellowstone National Park.

world's climate will change for many years. Monitoring of the area will, scientists hope, give sufficient warning to make preparations and evacuate the huge number of people in immediate danger.

▶▶ www.bbc.co.uk/science/horizon/1999/supervolcanoes.shtml

Volcanic activity at Yellowstone has remained relatively constant since scientists began monitoring it some 30 years ago.

INVESTIGATING THE EVIDENCE: HOW HUMANITY WAS NEARLY DESTROYED

The investigation:
Anthropologists study the history of the human race. They believe that around 73,000 years ago, humans almost became extinct. They want to find out whether the eruption of the Indonesian supervolcano Toba caused this catastrophe.

The scientists: Anthropologist Stanley H Ambrose of the University of Illinois, USA, has pieced together evidence from fieldwork in Kenya and elsewhere, with evidence from other studies.

Collecting the evidence:
By dating volcanic ash in archaeological sites in the Great Rift Valley, Professor Ambrose has been able to identify settlements in use just before the eruption of Toba. He has traced how people moved about and perhaps traded in the period just after the eruption.

The conclusion:
The eruption of Toba caused severe climate changes that probably killed all but 2,000–15,000 of the humans alive at the time. This trauma prompted the movement of people out of Africa to other areas of the world.

Hekla is a stratovolcano in the south of Iceland. It is the country's most active volcano, with more than 20 eruptions since 874 CE.

PREDICTION

Even if scientists can predict a volcanic eruption, there is nothing they can do to prevent it. In the past, there have been attempts to divert the flow of lava or mudslides away from towns and villages, or to trigger a small eruption in the hope of avoiding a larger one. However, volcanoes remain a law unto themselves, and our best hope is to have sufficient warning to move out of their way.

LESSONS FROM THE PAST

By examining the history of a volcano and its eruptions scientists can gain a good idea of whether it is likely to erupt in the near future. It is then the task of scientists carrying out careful monitoring and surveying to detect changes that mean an eruption is truly on the way.

▶▶ http://volcano.oregonstate.edu/
volcanologist/how_to.html

The investigation: The rate at which trees grow is affected by climate and reflected in their growth rings. Tree ring evidence can often be put together with other evidence to reveal past volcanic events.

The scientist: Dr Mike Baillie of Queen's University of Belfast, Northern Ireland, has examined growth rings in oak trees preserved in an Irish bog for evidence of a volcanic eruption around 2350 BCE.

Collecting the evidence: Dr Baillie found a band of ten very narrow rings, revealing slow growth in the trees from 2354–2345 BCE. This suggests an event that caused massive climate change. Carbon dating shows that a layer of fine volcanic debris from the Hekla 4 volcano in Iceland was laid down in peat bogs around 2310 BCE. Dr Baillie also looked at ancient records, which give an account of a disaster that laid the country waste for 30 years in around 2380 BCE.

The conclusion: The tree rings show that a huge eruption of Hekla 4 may have happened in 2354 BCE. This could have caused people to move to Ireland at the start of the Bronze Age. Pine trees disappeared a few years later, perhaps because they were cut down to fuel metal smelting.

READING THE SIGNS

A volcano is ready to erupt when the magma that collects underneath it reaches such a great pressure that it must burst out. Volcanologists can tell that the magma is moving upwards, ready to erupt, when the heat profile of the volcano changes, when more gas leaks from its fumaroles and when the sides of the mountain deform. But the more difficult task involves interpreting the signs to decide exactly when the eruption will occur – whether in weeks or only days – or whether the volcano will carry on growing and deforming for a few more years.

Tree rings can show how climate has affected the tree's growth rate, and and can suggest where volcanic activity has occurred.

The 5,000 inhabitants of this fishing port were evacuated before a 2km-long fissure opened in the southwest of the cone of the Helmaey volcano, Iceland, in 1973.

LIVING WITH DANGER

We have no choice but to live with the threat of volcanic eruptions. For most people, these are a distant worry. However, for those who live near volcanoes, they are an ever-present and frightening danger.

UNDER THE VOLCANO

In Tokyo in Japan, Naples in Italy and Washington in the USA, millions of people live close to volcanoes that are likely to erupt soon. These volcanoes are constantly watched and monitored for signs of change so that people can be evacuated if an eruption seems likely. People must be convinced that they are in real danger before they will leave, especially in poor, underdeveloped areas where evacuating could mean losing everything. In addition, evacuating people unnecessarily is expensive and disruptive, and means that the same people will be reluctant to leave the next time.

Plymouth on Montserrat in the Caribbean was destroyed by a pyroclastic flow in August 1997.

INVESTIGATING THE EVIDENCE: PLANNING FOR DISASTER

The investigation: A team of researchers developed an emergency-planning model for the city of Naples, Italy, which is in the shadow of the active volcano Vesuvius.

The scientists: A team from Cambridge University Centre for Risk in the Built Environment, UK, led by Robin Spence.

Collecting the evidence: An earlier study on the Caribbean island Montserrat showed that people are more likely to survive if hot ash is kept out of buildings during a pyroclastic flow, so looking at the openings of buildings was an important task. They used sophisticated modelling techniques to work out likely patterns of eruption and how they would affect people and buildings. They suggested possible evacuation strategies that could be put in place in advance in order to minimize deaths, injuries and disruption.

The conclusion: The findings, along with numerical models from the University of Pisa from previous pyroclastic flow events, have provided local services with the information they need to plan for evacuation, equip emergency services and design new buildings.

THE AFTERMATH

Not all volcanoes that could be dangerous are monitored. Around the Indian Ocean, there are many island and undersea volcanoes that could cause tsunami as well as eruption damage. When an eruption happens suddenly, without warning, thousands of people may die. Sometimes, a relatively small eruption triggers a more devastating and unexpected event such as a mudslide or tsunami. The best that we can do is send in rescue workers and emergency supplies to the area to support recovery work.

TOMORROW'S SCIENTISTS

Scientists use increasingly sophisticated instruments and techniques to measure the movement and changes in volcanoes around the world. Satellites watch more of our active volcanoes, and advanced computer-modelling systems show exactly what happened during past eruptions as well as what may occur in the future. Scientists are also looking beyond our planet for clues as to exactly what happens deep inside the Earth.

LOOKING BACK TO LOOK AHEAD

In volcanology, studying the past really is the key to understanding the future. By using advanced analysis and mathematics, along with the findings of field researchers such as geologists, seismologists and volcanologists, we can recreate in great detail some of the most violent eruptions in history. This helps us to create profiles for volcanoes that still erupt today. Using sophisticated computer models, scientists can predict in detail what a future eruption may be like and what the human cost could be.

VOLCANOES ON OTHER WORLDS

Earth is not the only planet with volcanoes. Space probes and telescopes have revealed volcanoes on other planets in our Solar System, and on some of their moons. Some function in a way similar to volcanoes on Earth, while others are quite different. Astronomers believe that vast ice volcanoes may have shaped the surfaces of Jupiter's moons Io, Europa and Ganymede. The volcanoes erupt liquid water, called cryomagma, which then freezes into huge plains of ice. Studying volcanoes on other planets gives scientists new insights into how Earth developed and how volcanism on our own planet works. As space exploration progresses, the horizons for volcanology will broaden even further.

Asbestos safety suits are essential wear for the volcanologists that brave the heat of active volcanoes to collect data and materials for analysis.

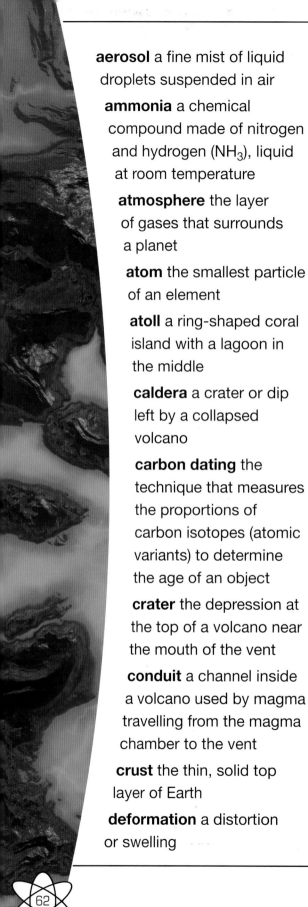

aerosol a fine mist of liquid droplets suspended in air

ammonia a chemical compound made of nitrogen and hydrogen (NH_3), liquid at room temperature

atmosphere the layer of gases that surrounds a planet

atom the smallest particle of an element

atoll a ring-shaped coral island with a lagoon in the middle

caldera a crater or dip left by a collapsed volcano

carbon dating the technique that measures the proportions of carbon isotopes (atomic variants) to determine the age of an object

crater the depression at the top of a volcano near the mouth of the vent

conduit a channel inside a volcano used by magma travelling from the magma chamber to the vent

crust the thin, solid top layer of Earth

deformation a distortion or swelling

dormant not currently erupting, but still capable of doing so

earthquake the shaking of the ground caused by Earth's tectonic plates moving against each other

ecosystem a community of living things in a specific location

erode to wear away by the action of the wind, water or ice

eruption an outpouring of a mixture of lava, gas and/or rock from a volcano

fault a crack in Earth's crust resulting from the movement of one side in relation to the other

fissure a long, narrow crack

fossil fuel a carbon fuel, such as coal, petroleum and natural gas, formed from the remains of prehistoric living things

geyser a vent that spurts water heated by underground magma at a very high temperature and pressure

GPS (Global Positioning System) a method of pinpointing a position on Earth through the use of satellites

hot spot the point at which magma rise up from the mantle, often in the middle of a tectonic plate, to form a volcano

inner core the very centre of Earth, made of solid metal at a very high temperature and pressure

isotope one of two or more atoms with the same atomic number but different atomic mass

lava the liquid rock that emerges from a volcano; the name for magma when it emerges

lava dome a small mound-like volcano that grows on the slopes or at the foot of a volcano

live describes a volcano that is capable of erupting

magma hot liquid rock from or within Earth's mantle

mantle the thick layer of semi-liquid molten rock that forms the middle layer of inner Earth, between the crust and the core

methane a gas made of carbon and hydrogen (CH_4), created when plant and animal matter are broken down

outer core the layer of superheated liquid metal under high pressure deep inside Earth. It surrounds the inner core, at the centre of Earth.

plateau a large, flat area of land

pumice a light, glassy, porous rock made of hardened lava

pyroclastic flow a fast-moving blast of rock fragments carried on a scorching wind from an eruption

rift zone an area on Earth where the tectonic plates are moving apart and magma wells up to the surface

sediment a layer of decayed plant and animal debris

sedimentary rock a type of rock created from sediment that is slowly compressed

seismic wave a wave of energy created when Earth is shaken by events such as earthquakes and volcanic eruptions

seismologist a person who measures and studies seismic waves

seismometer an instrument that measures seismic waves passing through Earth

species a genetically distinct type of plant, animal or microbe

subduction zone the area where the edge of one tectonic plate is pulled down below another plate

tectonic plate a slab of Earth's crust that moves slowly over the mantle, carrying continental land mass or ocean

tomography a technique for displaying the inside of a solid object using X-rays or ultrasound

vent the opening on the surface of a volcano where lava emerges

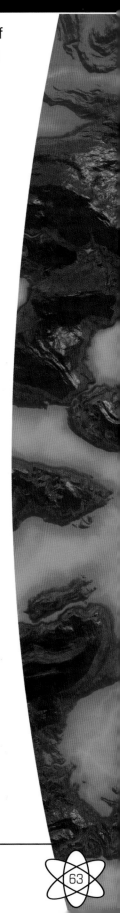